Also by Julie & John Hope
and published by Bantam

CHRISTMAS CAROLS FOR CATS
NURSERY RHYMES FOR CATS

CHRISTMAS CRACKERS FOR CATS

JULIE & JOHN HOPE

ILLUSTRATED BY SUE HELLARD

BANTAM BOOKS

LONDON · NEW YORK · TORONTO · SYDNEY · AUCKLAND

CHRISTMAS CRACKERS FOR CATS
A BANTAM BOOK: 0553 812963

First publication in Great Britain

PRINTING HISTORY
Bantam Books edition published 2000

1 3 5 7 9 10 8 6 4 2

Text copyright © Julie and John Hope 2000
Illustrations copyright © Sue Hellard 2000

The right of Julie and John to be identified as the authors of this work has been asserted in
accordance with sections 77 and 78 of the Copyright, Designs and Patents Act 1988

Condition of Sale
This book is sold subject to the condition that it shall not, by way of trade or otherwise, be lent, re-sold, hired out
or otherwise circulated in any form of binding or cover other than that in which it is published and without a
similar condition including this condition being imposed on the subsequent purchaser.

Bantam Books are published by Transworld Publishers,
61-63 Uxbridge Road, London W5 5SA,
a division of The Random House Group Ltd,
in Australia by Random House Australia (Pty)Ltd,
20 Alfred Street, Milsons Point, Sydney, NSW 2061, Australia,
in New Zealand by Random House New Zealand Ltd,
18 Poland Road, Glenfield, Auckland 10, New Zealand
and in South Africa by Random House (Pty) Ltd,
Endulini, 5a Jubilee Road, Parktown 2193, South Africa.

Reproduced, printed and bound in Singapore.

A kitty who stole food for leisure
Would hoard it all just like some treasure
But a fish on a plate
It acted as bait
Now he's awaiting Her Majesty's Pleasure

An Italian cat who ate jelly
Could not understand why his belly
Was so awfully round
That it rolled on the ground
And that's why his name is Pirelli

There was an old cat from Duluth
With one eye and hardly a tooth
Eats food with a paw
Drinks milk through a straw
Which makes her look rather uncouth

A wandering kitty called Romulus
Caught buses to add to his stimulus
They said he was fey
Never losing his way
And always got off at the terminus

(A cautionary tail!)

A vain Siamese who's called Peter
Was sitting too close to the heater
His tail it did smoke
But he made it a joke
Insisting his rear would look neater

Old Tom from the Mull of Kintyre
Decided that he would retire
Now the birds and the mice
Think it ever so nice
That he's sitting in front of the fire

A holiday junky called Grace
Would hide in her human's suitcase
And off she would fly
To Spain or Shanghai
It really was worth the disgrace

A cat who belonged to a priest
On communion wafers would feast
He'd drink up the wine
Until feeling benign
And bless every bird, mouse and beast

A raunchy old tomcat called Bertie
Had a mind that was ever so dirty
Now his goolies have gone
He's just one peeping Tom
So all he can do is get flirty

I'm a naughty old tomcat called Ming
Twice weekly I go on a fling
I'm so often smitten
I lose count of my kittens
Perhaps they should tie up my thing!

A cultural kitty called Strauss
Would visit the Grand Opera House
And wouldn't you know
His favourite show
Was the wonderful *Die Fledermaus*

A musical cat Salomé
Would listen to opera all day
And with her hind feet
She'd tap out the beat
To Verdi, Mozart and Bizet

A moggy who owned a TV
Would only watch wildlife on 3
And you haven't a hope
Of watching a soap
For he hides the remote up a tree

A theatrical kitty called Saul
Not wanting to hear a catcall
Got his friends from the press
The performance to bless
Now it's encores and fine caterwaul

A cat whose depression was chronic
Who blamed it on being Slavonic
Invented a draught
That made everyone laugh
And patented it as Cat-a-Tonic

A cat with great drive and ambition
Did study to be a magician
And he cast a great spell
So he could foretell
Each mouse and bird's present position

A foolish young cat from downtown
Would stare at the sky with a frown
He'd wait for a bird
Because he had heard
That what goes up always comes down

A celebrity kitty from Bude
Employed as a tester of food
For a large fee of course
A brand he'll endorse
He's not only famous but shrewd

A cat prodigy called Louise
Could play the piano with ease
Now she could be a star
But won't go too far
As she really can't reach all the keys

A lawyer who owned a prize bird
Under oath made his cat give his word
But while trying a case
The cat stuffed his face
For to swear before supper's absurd

A dirty old cat from Bilox
Would not let you clean his sand box
As the days they went by
The smell it got high
And now he's been sent for detox

A great British Blue cat called Beau
Got bored at a famous cat show
To help pass the time
He did chew on a line
And out all the lights they did go

A pedigree Persian from Goring
Thought judges at cat shows so boring
But I could be a winner
And I need to be thinner
So I'll hold in my tum while they're scoring

A fatcat who works as a model
Says trying to be thin is just twaddle
I'm the pride of catwalk
From Milan to New York
Who cares if I walk with a waddle

HUMPHREY: WHO LIVED OUT AT KEW
(Who was always polite and so gathered great prosperity)

The nicest cat that ever grew
Was Humphrey who lived out at Kew

He never lost his leather collar
Queens of the night he didn't foller
In eating fish he made no mess
And never clawed his human's dress

He liked, and when within his power
To wash his face upon the hour
And often, at the dinner table
Would beg as far as he was able
To give him if they did not mind
The chewiest morsels they could find

His later years were just as good
Shown promise of his kittenhood
In outdoor life he always tried
Avoiding rivals broad and wide

Inside the house he did aspire
To sit politely by the fire
And long before his thirteenth year
Had wedded
Gigi
What a gem!
From up the river (Henley-on-Thames)
And there they live in a stately house
Without a hint of rat or mouse
This shows what every cat just might
Become
By simply being polite

(*With apologies to Hilaire Belloc*)